HOW TO TALK TO PEOPLE

THE RIGHT WAY

The Only 7 Steps You Need to Master Conversation Skills, Effective Communication and Conversation Tactics Today

Dean Mack

© Copyright 2018 by Dean Mack. All rights reserved.

This document is geared towards providing exact and reliable information in regards to the topic and issue covered. The publication is sold with the idea that the publisher is not required to render accounting, officially permitted, or otherwise, qualified services. If advice is necessary, legal or professional, a practiced individual in the profession should be ordered.

From a Declaration of Principles which was accepted and approved equally by a Committee of the American Bar Association and a Committee of Publishers and Associations.

In no way is it legal to reproduce, duplicate, or transmit any part of this document in either electronic means or in printed format. Recording of this publication is strictly prohibited and any storage of this document is not allowed unless with written permission from the publisher. All rights reserved.

The information provided herein is stated to be truthful and consistent, in that any liability, in terms of inattention or otherwise, by any usage or abuse of any policies, processes, or directions contained within is the solitary and utter responsibility of the recipient reader. Under no circumstances will any legal responsibility or blame be held against the publisher for any reparation, damages, or monetary loss due to the information herein, either directly or indirectly.

Respective authors own all copyrights not held by the publisher.

The information herein is offered for informational purposes solely, and is universal as so. The presentation of the information is without contract or any type of guarantee assurance.

The trademarks that are used are without any consent, and the publication of the trademark is without permission or backing by the trademark owner. All trademarks and brands within this book are for clarifying purposes only and are the owned by the owners themselves, not affiliated with this document.

Table of Contents

Introduction

Learning how to talk effectively is important. Whether you want it or not, there is a constant flow of communication that happens everywhere. In fact, even if you choose not to talk, you still communicate a message to those around you. In the world today, communication remains as important as it has always been thousands of years ago. After all, before robots and computers can do their job, there must first be human interaction — and the best way to interact with another human being is by using effective communication techniques.

The following chapters will teach you everything that you need to know about mastering the art of talking to people and communicating effectively.

Chapter 1 lays down the basics, so that you will have a strong foundation and understanding of what effective communication is all about.

Chapter 2 reveals the 7 steps that you need to master the art of talking to people. This part of the book reveals what you need to learn to become a highly-effective communicator.

Chapter 3 discusses the best practices of effective communication. Learn additional tips and tricks that can further develop your communication skills.

May this book be your guiding light to success and a happier life.

Chapter 1: The Basics

What is effective communication?

Being able to communicate is a vital element of humanity. The history of communication can be traced back to the time when warriors would form a circle around a bonfire and exchange stories with one another. Today, there are so many ways and means to communicate: You can send a text message, write an email, make a phone call, and others. Still, nothing beats face-to-face communication as being the most personal and effective manner of talking with another human being.

There are many definitions of what communication is. According to Merriam Webster's Dictionary, communication is "the act or process of using words, sounds, signs, or behaviors to express or exchange information or to express your ideas, thoughts, feelings, etc., to someone else." Simply put, communication is about expressing yourself to another person. It is worth noting that many people know how to communicate — even a baby communicates with her parents. However, only a few know how to communicate effectively, in a way that people will really hear and understand what you are trying to express. This book is about *effective* communication, which is about being able to communicate your thoughts, feelings, and ideas, clearly and more effectively. This is about having a real conversation with another human being.

Is it important to learn effective communication? This is a legitimate question. After all, most people do not know how to communicate effectively and merely say whatever ideas they may have in mind, so why would anyone bother to learn effective communication? Of course, you are free to decide whether or not you want to take the effort to learn how to talk effectively. You can stay the way that you are right now, but you can also improve your communication skills and see the significant and positive difference that it can do to your life.

People who know how to communicate effectively tend to be more successful in life. They are also the ones who establish a good network of connections. This is because human beings like people who communicate clearly and effectively. Take note that this is not just about having a conversation, but effective communication also means making the other person feel good about having a conversation with you. As you can see, true effective communication is not just about expressing your thoughts and ideas to another. It goes beyond the simple definition of what communication is all about and also takes into consideration the whole communication process, as well as the entire experience of having a conversation.

Have you noticed people who seem to be able to command a whole audience just by talking? How about people who are able to carry on a conversation for hours yet still capture the attention and interest of his audience? These people are the ones who communicate effectively. Of course, effective communication does not just work before a crowd of people. It also works powerfully in a one-on-one conversation setup. These days, many people have the habit of communicating; however, they do not do so effectively. In fact, many people are poor communicators and barely manage to get a message across clearly. If you learn and practice the techniques in this book that will turn you into a real effective communicator, then you can set yourself apart and have your own brand. People will like talking with you. In fact, they will like you as a person. This, of course, can open lots of doors of opportunity. Learning to communicate effectively can change your life, as well as the life of the people you talk to. It simply has its own magic that can create a positive impact.

The communication process

The communication process refers to a process whereby two or more people exchange information. Take note that it is an *exchange* of information and not just about sending information to another. Hence, it is a two-way process where the parties take turns to talk and listen to each other.

The communication process has 6 parts or elements. Let us take a look at them one by one:

➢ Sender

The sender is the one that starts the communication process. The sender is also referred to as the *source*. The sender has an information, thought, or idea, or even an emotion that he would like to share to another. In order to do this, he will have to encode the message in a form that will be understood by another, and then transmit the message.

➢ Receiver

Once the message of a sender is transmitted, it is directed to a receiver, or the person to whom the sender is talking to and to whom he wishes to convey the said information. Once the receiver receives the message coming from the sender, he will then have to decode it. This is the reason why the language used by the sender should be something that the receiver understands so that he (the receiver) will easily be able to decode the message and understand what the sender is trying to express.

> Message

Obviously, this refers to the information that the sender wants to communicate to the receiver. If you combine the sender, receiver, and the message, altogether, then you have the most basic elements of a communication process. However, the process does not really end there.

> Medium

The medium is also referred to as the *channel*. It simply refers to the means that the sender uses to send his message. For example, a text message can be sent using a mobile phone as the medium.

> Feedback

At the basic level a communication is complete once the sender is able to transmit his message and the said message is receiver by the receiver. However, it is not the end of the process. Once the receiver has received the message, he then responds to the sender. This is to indicate that he has received and understood the message. A feedback usually keeps the communication process active and on-going. It can be verbally made or even in writing. It can even be expressed through one's actions.

➢ Other factors

The communication process is also subject to other elements that may affect how the information is sent, received, and understood:

Noise - A noise usually comes in the form of interference that makes the information difficult to be understood. It can refer to the actual noise in the environment which makes it hard for the receiver to even hear the voice of the sender, or it can also refer to the static interference when communication over the phone. Anything that hinders the communication process may be considered a noise.

Context - The context by which something is transmitted can affect how the other person would understand it. This, of course, can affect the quality of the exchange of information. This may have some social and cultural aspect into it. Hence, before you transmit any message, be sure to do so in the right context in order to avoid misunderstanding. For example, to the Chinese, calling them as *intsik*, which is just another term for *Chinese*, is considered insulting. Hence, when you are talking with a Chinese person, do not include the word *intsik* when you transmit a message; otherwise, the receiver might feel insulted even if you are saying something pleasant.

Time element - Time can also be considered another factor. This refers to the time when the receiver gets to receive or read the message transmitted by the sender. This normally applies in cases where you are not engaged in a face-to-face conversation. For example, when you communicate via email or text messaging. You cannot always be sure that the receiver will be able to get your message immediately after you send it.

It is worth noting that effective communication means so much more than knowing the communication process. Being aware of this process is only good in order to help you understand how a communication normally takes place, but being a truly effective communicator means so much more than knowing how the process works. This, however, can give you a good idea on how you can communicate more effectively.

Is it for you?

Many people are aware of the term *effective communication*, but only a few are truly able to communicate effectively. So, is it for you? The good news is that effective communication is for everyone. This is because anyone can learn it. However, just like anything that is worth learning, you will need to dedicate your time and efforts to it. This is not something that you can just learn overnight. It takes practice and commitment to become an effective communicator, but it is nevertheless learnable and doable.

The following chapters will walk you through the 7 steps that will turn you into an effective communicator. If you stick to these steps and practice them continuously, then you will soon be able to learn and even master the art of effective communication. If you are a complete beginner who is just starting out, then do not expect to be able to master the following steps quickly and easily. But, if you persist in your practice, then these steps will get easier over time. Soon, they will become second nature to you. Allow these steps to become a part of you, and you will be able to do them smoothly and naturally.

So, is effective communication for you? The answer is *yes*, and it is well within your reach. The secrets to learning the art of effective communication and conversation are revealed in the pages of this book. Just keep your determination strong, never stop learning, and keep on practicing. This book will give you the knowledge that you need; it is up to you to turn it into actual practice.

Why would anyone want to learn how to talk to people effectively? If you stop for a while and notice what is going on around you, it is easy to recognize that the "machinery" of how the world works is mainly based on how people talk with one another. Gone are the days when swords and steel had to do the talking. In the modern world, people just talk to set things in motion. Whether you are in a workplace environment, in school, or even just in the comfort of your home, it is talking with one another that connects people. It is also how ideas, feelings, and thoughts are usually expressed. Hence, if you learn how to talk to people effectively, then just imagine the benefits that you can enjoy. You will be able to express your ideas more accurately; you can even influence people with your words; you can be a better negotiator; you can make people open up to you; you can build good relationships with people, and so much more. The possibilities become limitless. This is because you will be able to talk and connect with people on a deeper level. And, as you may already know, once you establish this kind of connection with people, then chances are that you can work together mutually and more effectively. Talking effectively with people is probably one of the best things to experience in life, and it can also open lots of opportunities for you.

Chapter 2: The 7 Steps

#1 Prepare

Preparation can go a long way. In fact, if you have enough preparation, then you could almost guarantee being able to talk effectively. But, how do you prepare? This is where the problem usually is. Many people know the importance of doing preparation, but only a few are able to do *sufficient* preparation.

If you know that you will be talking with someone, the first step that you should do is to prepare for the meeting. Know as much about the person whom you will be talking to. Find out about his interests, if possible. Although communication is about voicing out your thoughts and ideas, an important part of effective communication is to know about the other person. This should be part of your preparation. This is like preparing for a date. This will ensure that you can keep the other person interested in conversing with you. By talking about the other person's interest, you can make the other person happy talking with you. A common mistake made by beginners is to prepare only for the things that they want to say, without making any preparation for meeting the other person. Take note that you are dealing with another human being and not just someone who will listen and receive whatever you want to say.

There are no hard and fast rules on how you should prepare. The manner and amount of preparation that you need will depend on the circumstances of the situation. So, for example, you will be meeting with a business tycoon. Find out and research what his business is all about. If he is engaged in the stock market, then try to learn interesting things about the stock market. Also learn the current trend and happenings in the stock market. One way to communicate effectively is to talk about something that the other person is interested in.

Another part of your preparation is to expect the topics and subtopics that will be brought up during the actual meeting. It is important for you to have a good understanding of the subject matter so that you can give insightful and meaningful opinions. If you do not have a good grasp of the subject matter, then it will be hard to communicate anything worthwhile to the other person. One of the things that you should keep in mind is that effective communicators have mastery or at least a respectable amount of knowledge of what they are talking about. Hence, subject mastery should be part of your preparation.

How do you know if you have prepared enough for the meeting? It is quite hard to tell if the amount of preparation that you have is already enough or not, because a conversation can lead to so many things. But, ideally, you should be able to discuss the subject matter easily and smoothly. If you reach a point that talking and discussing the details of a particular topic is easy for you to do, then you are more likely to be ready to engage in an actual conversation. Of course, this means having a good amount of knowledge, and this knowledge can come from your preparation. Thanks to the Internet, you always have an access to a vast network of information. This will allow you to do your research in the comfort of your home. You may also want to read books and talk with and interview experts on the subject. This way you will be able to gain as much information that you need. Knowledge is important because if you do not know the subject matter of a conversation well, then it will be difficult for you to say something good and meaningful about it.

Another part of preparation is the physical preparation. It is a good practice to dress properly for the occasion. If you know that you are properly dressed and look decent enough, then you will be more confident to face and talk with other people. Needless to say, you need to be confident when you talk. If you are not confident, then people will find it difficult to trust you and believe whatever you say. You do not have to dress formally except, of course, if the situation requires it. However, you should always look presentable.

Unfortunately, you will not always be given time to make preparations. There are times when you will just find yourself in a conversation without any prior preparation. In this case, you can rely on other techniques as revealed in this book in order to keep the conversation effective and interesting. Of course, being able to prepare is a good advantage, so be sure to make use of it whenever possible.

#2 Listen

It is worth noting that effective communication is a two-way process. Unfortunately, many peoples think communication is just about being the one who is talking. This is wrong. From time to time, you should also be the one who is on the receiving end. One of the most important elements of effective communication is listening. To be more specific, this refers to *active listening*. It is unfortunate that although the importance of listening is a common advice, many people still fail to observe it. Keep in mind that listening means so much more than just hearing the other person's voice. When you listen, you should *understand* what the other person is saying. Another advice is to react to what the other person tells you. Giving a response ensures the other person that you are attentive to him and that you understand what he is saying.

There are certain differences between listening and active listening. Most people only know how to listen but they do not do it actively. So, how do you do active listening? When you actively listen to a person, you do not just hear his words. You should also ask questions and make appropriate responses to what the other person is telling you. Asking questions and reacting ensure the other person that he has your attention and that you are able to follow his train of thoughts. This is active listening. Listening, on the other hand, simply refers to hearing what the other person is telling you. Unfortunately, most people just know how to listen and do not make the other person feel that attention that you are actually giving him. When you actively listen to another, it will tend to make him feel loved and understood. Try talking to someone who actively listens to every word you say and you will know just how comforting it is to have someone to just talk to even if you do not get any solution to a problem. Indeed, many people are not really looking for a solution; they just want to have someone who would sincerely listen to them, someone who would hear whatever they say without judging them. Surprisingly, although this may seem an easy thing to do, most people are too preoccupied to even listen to another human being. Most of the time if they know that they would not gain anything from the conversation, they would rather avoid meeting the person. This book teaches its readers to value the existence and life of another person. Do not forget that the best time to talk with people effectively is not when you have something important to say, but when people actually want to talk with someone — and that someone could be you.

Do not commit the common mistake of being too self-centered. You should also take the time to hear and listen to what the other person has to say. If you are not willing to listen then it would be better for you to just talk with yourself. Remember: True effective communication is a two-way process. Before you even talk to somebody, be sure that you are also ready to listen. Unfortunately, many people become sort of narcissistic when they engage in conversation. They are too concerned with themselves that they fail to hear what the other person is telling them. Keep in mind that if you want to be a good communicator, then you should be a good listener.

Is it important for the other person to know that you are listening to him? The answer is *yes*. A common mistake committed by lots of people is to listen to a person without making him feel that they can hear him out. Take note that the person would not know that you can understand him unless you make positive responses. If the other person feels that you are actively listening to him, then you will more easily gain his trust, and he will feel more comfortable opening up to you. However, if the person feels that you are not giving him enough attention, then it would be hard to make him open up to you. Soon, he will feel very uncomfortable and even feel insulted if you do not make him feel that you are listening to him. So, how do you assure the other person that you are actively listening to him? Of course, you will not tell him, "Hey, I am listening to you." Rather, you will make him feel that you are actually listening to him while he is talking to you. You can easily do this by observing some simple practices like making eye contact and asking follow-up questions. For example, if a person says, "I am sad." ask him why he is sad. You cannot always expect people to open up to you immediately. Most of the time, you first need to make them feel that you want to listen to them and that you are someone whom they can trust. Once they feel how sincere you are and once they are comfortable enough talking with you, then that is the time when they will be more open to you. As you can see, the art of effective communication is not just about expressing your thoughts and ideas clearly, but is also about helping other people to express their thoughts and feelings and to share them with you.

Everyone will tell you that making eye contact is important. But, what if you find it uncomfortable to look at a person's eyes as you talk/listen? A good way to solve this problem is too look at the edge of his eye. This way, it will seem as if you are staring right at him. Another trick is to stare at the bridge of his nose right between his eyes. Of course the best way would still be to get used to looking at a person's eyes when you talk. Just practice it with every person you interact with, and you will soon get used to it. If you are truly sincere and would like to listen to another person, looking at his eyes would come naturally. As they say, "The eyes are the windows to the window."

From time to time, you may have to deal with people who are simply hard to listen to. Usually, these people are those who talk too much and simply have difficulty in expressing themselves clearly. Worse, they tend to talk loudly. So, how do you deal with these people? The principle remains the same: You have to listen. Now, if you find it hard to listen to everything that they are saying because you know that much of the things they are talking about do not really matter, the key is simply to identify keywords. You have to be patient with these people. You may find it irritating to listen to everything that they say, so a good tip is to just identify the real issue and ignore the others. Once you know the main issue, then you can always make an appropriate response. Sad to say, there are some people who have to talk for minutes just to say something that can be expressed in a few seconds. Again, effective communication teaches you to be good and respectable at all times.

You should also realize and appreciate that listening is an act of love and/or kindness. When you listen to another, you give him your time and attention. This is the kind of sincerity that people want. Needless to say, when somebody talks with you, you should stop whatever it is that you are doing and put your focus on the person who is talking. This is also the time to make eye contact with the person to assure him that you are listening to him.

A common mistake is to think that the person you are talking to is looking for a solution to a problem. The truth is that most people who talk about their problems are not really looking for a solution, but are merely looking for someone who would listen to them and understand them. Of course, the way to do this is by listening to the person who has a problem. These people simply want to be heard and understood. Unfortunately, many of these people feel that they are alone in the world, and so having someone who could listen and understand them would make them feel less alone. As you can see, the art of listening is a very important skill that you should master. In fact, expert communicators agree that listening is more important, if not as important, as talking. It is also by listening actively that you will be able to know how to best respond to a person. The more that you listen and understand a person, the easier it will be to connect with him on a deeper level.

#3 Ask the right questions

Learning to ask the right questions is a vital element of effective communication. It is also by asking questions that you can get to expound and deepen the level of conversation. It directs the flow of the conversation. By asking questions, you also assure the other person that you are actively listening to him and that you are able to follow his thoughts. However, do not be like other people who ask questions just for the sake of asking. Rather, every question that you ask must serve some purpose. A good advice is to ask only responsive questions. These are the questions that will get the story forward and develop the flow of conversation. For example, if a person says, "I took the bar exams." Ask him how he prepared for the exams and how he feels about them. This will definitely give you lots of information that you can use to further develop the level of conversation. By asking questions, you do not just make the person feel that you are listening to him, but it also encourages a person to talk more and open up to you. Needless to say, you should ask questions in a natural and gentle manner, and do not make the other person feel as if he were in some kind of investigation.

By asking questions, you make the other person feel that you are open to whatever it is that he has to say. Once again, effective communication is not just about you expressing your own thoughts and opinions. More importantly, it is about being open to other people and listening to whatever they have to say. Do not worry; you will also get your time to talk and share your own opinions.

Asking questions is also an excellent way to understand the other person. You should understand that effective communication is founded upon mutual respect and understanding. You need to understand each other. From time to time, you may have to tackle a sensitive topic where you may share different and even conflicting views. When you use effective communication, you can still talk about such matters without sacrificing peace and harmony between/among the parties. As the saying goes, "You can agree to disagree without sounding disagreeable." When you ask questions, you should also be ready to face answers that you may find unacceptable, but you need to learn to respect the other person. If you cannot respect a certain view or opinion, at least respect the other party as a person. After all, you are never obliged to adapt the same mindset or viewpoint. Indeed, from time to time, it is also important to appreciate the beauty in diversity.

Asking questions is one thing, asking the *right* questions is another. Expert communicators make sure to ask only the questions that will help develop a conversation. When you ask a question, that is the time when the other person will be expected to open up and share with you something, depending on your question. Be careful with the questions that you ask. Do not ask questions that would insult or offend the other person. If he feels that you are insulting him with your question then he will be more defensive, which will prevent you from having a meaningful conversation.

Most of the time, you only have to help the other person open up to you by asking him questions. For example, if a person says that he attended an event, ask him about the event. He will then tell you details about it. If you want to know more, then ask him more specific questions based on the information that he has also revealed to you. Simply stated, you only have to guide the person to share with you the whole story by asking him questions. This is the beauty of asking questions: You get to know more about the other person, and all that you need to do is ask.

#4 Share

Talking is sharing. Effective communication is about sharing and expressing yourself to people. Of course, you are expected to share something that the other person will like or at least find interesting.

But, what can you share? Every person has a story to tell. If not a story, then ideas, thoughts, opinions, and feelings that they can share with the world. Simply put, there is always something that you can share. The good thing about this is that you can share almost anything and everything that you want. However, effective communication is not just about sharing, but sharing something that the other person can also relate and connect to.

Do not underestimate the power of telling a good story. As they say, "Ideas come and go; stories stay." Sometimes it is most effective to tell whatever it is that you want to say in a narrative format. Stories usually have a way of expressing ideas more clearly. There is also power in stories that makes them hard to forget. Hence, you might want to use some storytelling when communicating effectively.

When you engage in a conversation, you should also expect for the other person to share something with you. You will have to take turns as to who will be the sender and the receiver, especially when telling a story. Do not worry; in every effective communication both or all parties will be given the chance the talk and share something. This is one of the things that set apart effective communication from just any other form of communication. Usually, when people think of the word *communication*, they only understand it to be a one-way process where you just have to talk whatever is on your mind. Worse, people usually do this carelessly without being careful of their choice of words. Hence, it is easy to understand why many people are not effective communicators.

When you share, you should also be open to feedbacks. After sharing something, you will most likely get a response from the receiver. Now, whatever response you get, remind yourself to remain calm and respectful. If you come to think of it, although it may seem that how a person responds is outside of your control, you actually have some control over it. This is because you can expect how a statement or story that you share would make the other person think or feel about it. For example, if you mention your recent success in life, then you can expect for your friend to be happy for you. Hence, before you share something, it is a good practice to pause for a moment and reflect how it would appear to the person with whom you want to tell it.

Effective communication aims to be able to build an environment and relationship based on trust where the parties are free to share everything with each other. This is one of the best things about learning effective communication. It also takes into account the relationship that you build with the other person. It is not just about expressing an idea, feeling, or thought. It also focuses on building good relationships.

When you share, especially when you share your weakness, it makes the other person feel that you can be trusted since you are the one who even reveal your vulnerability. People like honesty and openness. The only reason that usually prevents them for being open is because of some trust issue. But, if you take the initiative and be the one to remove your own walls and share, you can rest assured that it will be appreciated. Most of the time, it will make the other party feel that you are someone whom he can trust and rely on. Needless to say, you also have to be careful with what you share, especially if it is related to business or your profession.

Sharing can be a wonderful experience, especially if you know that the other person is sincere about it. When you share something, you give and entrust a part of you to another. In the same way, when a person shares something with you, you also receive something from him, perhaps an information, a secret, a story, or otherwise. The point is that when a person shares something, a connection is made. Now, it is only how you handle and respond to it which will determine if the connection is still worth having or not. Effective communicators know that value of sharing and respect whatever they receive from other people. Since they respect people regardless of their views, people also respect them. Never forget that effective communication is about building a good relationship. There is no reason to argue with one another. You only have to share and listen, and be respectful at all times.

The moment that you decide to talk to another, it is also a decision to finally be open to another human being. A common obstacle that prevents people from sharing or opening up to another is shyness. You need to understand that you should not allow shyness to prevent you from connecting with another person. Remember: As long as you are honest, then you do not have to be shy. If you focus on being shy, then you only make it stronger. If you continuously allow shyness to prevent you from having a good conversation, then you will not be able to experience the beauty of connecting with another person. Also, if you really feel uncontrollably shy, just remember that you are talking to just another human being. Feeling shy is normal. The best way to overcome shyness is by exposing yourself to more people. Soon, you will get used to it, and you will be more confident.

#5 Gestures

"Actions speak louder than words." Learn to use gestures effectively. Another thing that you should learn is how to read gestures. Also learn to understand facial expressions. Learning to use the right gestures is a good way to better illustrate your point, as well as to keep the conversation alive and interesting. Learning to read gestures will allow you to understand another person more clearly even before he says a word, or even when he says something that totally contradicts the truth. Gestures would reveal to you information that otherwise may be hidden from you. In fact, many people do not even realize how much information they share with others simply from their gestures. If you learn to understand the meaning behind the gestures, then you may be able to start reading people like a book. This means being more understanding of them.

It is also worth noting that not all gestures may signify a clear meaning. For example, some people associate a certain movement to mean that the person is lying. However, just because you see another person doing it does not mean that the said person is lying. This is where reading gestures can be tricky. However, it is still beneficial to know and understand the different gestures and their possible meanings. Although you cannot rely solely on gestures in understanding people, they can, nonetheless, still give you good insights not just about the subject matter of the conversation but also about the person with whom you are talking to.

One of the effective communicators who used gestures was Adolf Hitler. Yes, even Hitler knew the power of gestures that he studied his own gestures and learned to apply them more effectively. Feel free to learn the different gestures, as well as how you can apply them. There are helpful gestures that you can easily learn and use. These gestures can help you to illustrate a point more effectively and make the conversation more interesting. Of course, gestures alone are not enough. You should also communicate something that has meaning and value.

Learning to use gestures is a good way to be an effective communicator as it will also allow you to express your idea more clearly. It is also worth noting that gestures come naturally. However, there are those that have been used by humanity for ages that people associate them with a corresponding meaning. For example, closing your arms signify that you are taking a defensive position. However, some people simply like to cross their arms even for no reason. Hence, it is also good to know the meaning behind the gestures, so that you can correctly avoid using certain gestures that may cause misunderstanding and confusion, as well as to be able to get information from people even without talking directly to them. This will allow you to be able to understand people more effectively.

It can be stressing that gestures do not always mean what people say that they signify, hence, just because a person looks away after you ask him a question does not always mean that he is lying to you. Some people simply respond differently from the normal. A good way to know if your understanding of a certain gesture is correct or not is by testing it. After some time, you will get used to this to the point that you can tell if a specific gesture really intends to convey the meaning that has been associated with it or simply just a coincidence. This is something that comes with practice. One thing is sure: Learning about gestures can get you one step ahead of the conversation. If your job is something that requires convincing people and/or something that requires you to understand other people more completely, then learning to read gestures is something that should be in your arsenal. Although reading gestures is not always 100% accurate, it can, nonetheless, give you valuable insights which can be helpful.

Using gestures is also an excellent way to keep the conversation alive and interesting. Imagine talking to someone who does nothing but talk without using any gesture. Soon enough, you will surely get bored listening to him even if he is saying something interesting. Proper use of gestures can add action to the conversation, which will give it more life.

A common mistake is to use the same gesture over and over again. Most people who are not aware of effective communication simply allow themselves to use gestures unconsciously. Although gestures usually just happen even if you do not give it any thought, you will most likely be using the same gesture over and over again if you just allow it to express itself naturally. When this happens, your movement can look monotonous, and this may not look good to the person who is listening to you. Therefore, it is also a good advice for you to know the different gestures and then try to use them when you talk. A good way to practice with gestures is to watch yourself in the mirror as you talk. Pay attention to how you move and the gestures that you make. Also take note of your facial expressions, as well as how you project yourself. Make sure to use gestures naturally. Forcing to use a certain gesture may make you look awkward, so be sure to apply every gesture smoothly and in accordance with the thought or emotion that you are trying to convey.

#6 Trust

You need to remember that effective communication is based on trust. If the person you are talking with trusts you enough, then he will be more open to you. The more open and honest a conversation is, the more meaningful it will be. But, how do you make people trust you? You should understand that effective communication does not use deception. It is not about manipulating the other person. Rather, effective communication creates a bond of trust and confidence because you are worthy of being trusted. The key to this is sincerity. Unfortunately, some people think that they have to use tricks, deception, and lies to be an effective communicator. This is not true. In fact, although such lies may work to your advantage for some time, they will soon ruin your reputation in the long run. Hence, your focus should be on building a good relationship with people.

If you pay attention to the techniques in this book, as well as in other books, you will notice that the techniques are not really out of the ordinary, such as making eye contact, asking questions, and others. They are simply what a kind, decent, and sincere person would do if engaged in a conversation with someone whom he deeply cares about. Effective communication makes you to be that person. This is one of the reasons why learning to communicate effectively can change a person. The art of effective communication teaches one how to act as a gentleman or a kind and loving person.

It is usual for people to have walls as a form of defensive mechanism. After all, these days, it is hard to find people whom you can trust completely. However, these walls can be a barrier to an effective communication. You probably recognized these walls when you talk to someone who seems very reserved and does not open up to you. When this happens, the tendency is for you to be the one to do all the talking, which is not good. Although it is still considered communication, it is not *effective* communication. Again, communication is a two-way process. So, how do you make such kind of people to open up to you? An effective way is to show the person that it is okay to bring down his/her walls. To do this, you have to take the initiative and bring down your own walls to show the person that it is safe not to have any defenses. Show him your own vulnerability. In other words, trust the other person, and show him that you trust him. Most of the time, when you do this, the other person will appreciate your efforts and initiative and will start to lower his walls and begin to open up to you as well. When this happens, you can now engage in a more meaningful conversation.

When people study how to communicate with people more effectively, they often focus on themselves, specifically on how to express their thoughts and ideas more effectively. Although this is part of effective communication, the process does not end there. Unfortunately, they fail to realize that the person they are talking to are not effective communicators. Hence, instead of just focusing on yourself and what you have to say, you can have a more meaningful conversation by also helping the other person in expressing his thoughts, feelings, and ideas. When a person feels that it is easy and comfortable talking with you, then you will be able to gain his trust.

In our world today full of shrewd people who seek only for their own gain, it is not easy to find someone with whom you can talk about everything and feel good for doing so. This book teaches you how to be that person, and how you can turn a simple conversation into something that is meaningful and memorable.

Trust is important. If you have bad intentions, then this book is not for you. To make the other person trust you, then you should be worthy of being trusted. Usually, a good way to show the other person your own vulnerability is by showing him your own weaknesses. Normally, people will tend to be more open once they know that you are already being open to them. So, take the initiative and the risk and bring down your own walls first. Sometimes in order to be trusted, you need to be the first one to trust someone.

It is also important not to break a person's trust. Hence, be sure to always be true to your words and do not resort to any falsehood. Also, if a person has entrusted you with a secret, make sure to keep it a secret forever. Trust, once broken, is almost impossible to restore. Take very good care of it.

#7 Be more connected

This is the part where you deepen the level of conversation and get more connected. Normally, this part happens on its own and is simply about observing the aforesaid techniques continuously. This is mainly about building a stronger relationship. Talking to a person does not usually happen just once. If you get to feel comfortable with each other, then you will most likely meet up again and talk some more. In fact, if you come to think of it, the relationships in the world share the very same activity: talking. It is by talking with one another that people negotiate things. It is also how people share thoughts and ideas on a regular basis. Hence, if you want to be more connected, then it would mean having more conversations with the same person or persons. This is simply how the world works: People get connected by talking with one another.

When you talk with people, a suggested approach is to consider every person that you talk to as special. It does not matter whether you are talking with your boss at work, a colleague, friend, spouse, or any one at all. The key is to see everyone as special and to treat them in a special way. Sadly, people have already forgotten just how meaningful talking should be. This is exactly why learning how to talk effectively is important, especially in today's world where people easily take things for granted.

It is important for you to realize what it really means to *talk*. If done with sincerity and kindness, talking creates a connection that can go beyond the physical. Have you experienced having a soulful connection with someone? This can be achieved through effective communication. Once people trust each other and become more open, other positive energies like love, kindness, hope, and even happiness, can be channeled through talking — and this can create a truly meaningful and powerful bond.

Repeated meetings and talks can make a bond or relationship much stronger. Of course, you are expected to continuously apply the techniques as revealed in this book. As you can see by now, these techniques are not something that you apply today and forget tomorrow. Rather, they become *you*. Perhaps this is one of the reasons why some people find it hard to communicate effectively: They are not sincere enough to do it. To talk effectively, you cannot just fake being sincere or listening to people. You should be truly sincere and actually listen to whatever they tell you. This is something that you cannot just act out intentionally. If you are not sincere enough, then the other person will most likely feel your insincerity. How can you look at a person in the eyes and say that you care if you do not feel like caring at all? Hence, if you want to turn yourself into an effective communicator, you should also improve yourself as a person. Self-improvement is part of the process.

The more connected you are to a person, the more the communication will deepen. This is another reason why you should not fake being sincere; it is because it would not last long. If you are not true enough, then the other person will soon recognize it. You should also realize that even if you talk effectively, it does not guarantee that anyone would love to talk with you. After all, talking effectively does not mean pleasing or entertaining everyone whom you talk with. Hence, do not expect for people to flock around you and like you for being an effective communicator. Rather, just know that by learning these techniques, you will be able to connect more intimately with people, and that this art of talking would make you a better human being.

Chapter 3: Best Practices

Learn from the experts

When learning to communicate effectively, you will most likely try to learn from experts who claim to have mastered the art of effective communication. Feel free to visit their blogs and read their books on the subject. However, just be careful, because not everyone who claims to be an expert in effective communication is a real expert. In today's world, it is fairly easy to promote one's self as an expert in anything. Therefore, take whatever you read or hear with a grain of salt. The best way to know if a certain technique actually works is by testing it.

Although it is good to learn from experts, it is strongly suggested that you do not depend on them completely. Do not forget that effective communication is an art. Therefore, you should also develop your own style of conversing with people.

It is also a good idea to closely study how the real experts communicate. For example, play a certain video and pay attention to how an expert talks, his gestures, how he uses pauses, tone of voice, and others.

A good way to learn from experts is by watching their videos. You might want to try YouTube for this. Pay attention to how these "experts" talk and get a message across very clearly. It is also advised that you videos of famous orators and observe how they deliver their message powerfully. Take note of their choice of words, voice, posture and gestures, as well as the way that they project themselves to the audience. Orators are usually great communicators who are able to deliver a message powerfully. Of course, their techniques may not always be applicable to a day-to-day conversation, but you can still learn from them, especially from the way they use words to express their thoughts and emotions.

Find your voice

You need to find your voice as early as possible. Usually, a beginner will try to imitate how an expert talks. This is not a good approach. The thing is that no matter how hard you try, you cannot completely duplicate another person's style of talking with people. Instead, what you should do is to develop your own style by using your own voice.

Finding your own voice takes trial and error. Many times it is knowing what your voice *is not* that will lead you to find the voice that is truly your own. Every person has his or her own voice. Take note that this does not refer to your literal *voice*, but is rather something about the way you connect with other people. It is also something that you develop as you continue to practice effective communication.

Effective communication is an art. There are many ways to apply the same techniques. To help you find your voice, you can try to adapt different styles of communicating and see which one best suits your personality. The best way to know your unique voice is to just be yourself. Do not think about being successful or being an effective communicator. Simply be yourself and talk naturally. Of course, this does not mean that you should be careless in your approach. However, it should be noted that aside from applying the techniques, it is also important to be yourself when you talk.

Talk clearly

When you talk, make sure that you pronounce all the words clearly. Some people tend to "eat" their words or talk too fast. Help the receiver to understand your message by conveying it in a clear and easy-to-understand manner. A good advice to be able to talk more clearly is to talk slowly and make sure that you pronounce all the words clearly and correctly. Also, be as concise as possible. Avoid using statements that are too wordy. Avoid unnecessary words and go straight to the point.

If you have problems with stammering, then a good way to avoid or at least lessen such problem is by talking more slowly. Now, it takes practice to do this, especially if you are used to talking too fast. However, this is something that you can easily learn with continuous practice. The key is to always remind yourself to talk clearly. A common mistake is only to practice it when you need it. What you should do is to make it a part of your day-to-day conversations. Keep in mind that how you talk in your day-to-day conversations will most likely be the way you talk when you attend meetings, events, and others. Also, effective communication embraces all forms of conversations, so it is only right that you apply the techniques every time you engage in any conversation, including the usual day-to-day talks that you engage in.

You should also learn how to regulate your voice. Learn when to use a high tone and a low tone, also learn when to whisper. If you observe expert communicators, you will notice how they play with their voice and use it strategically. They project their voice powerfully and deliver the message that they want to get across very clearly. Also, being too monotonous can be boring, so regulate your voice and avoid following a single rhythm.

Be flexible

Effective communication requires one to be flexible enough. Hence, it does not have any fixed rule to follow. How you approach a subject will most likely depend on the circumstances of a situation. It is also worth noting that you cannot always expect to talk with someone who shares the same view as you have. Hence, you should also be flexible enough to welcome other points of view.

Depending on the person with whom you are talking to, you may also have to adjust how you talk from time to time. This is not about being untrue to yourself, but merely for the sake of being more effective. After all, you cannot expect for everyone to respond in the same way. If a certain technique does not work on a certain person, then you might want to try another technique in its place.

Being flexible also refers to the ability of controlling yourself. Sometimes you may have to control your reaction and choice of words. Do not forget that part of effective communication is learning how to make the other person feel more respected and comfortable. Of course, being flexible does not mean that you should aim to please the other person. It bears stressing that you are not obliged in any way to please the other person. There is a difference between pleasing another person and allowing him to be more comfortable with you.

Not everyone will respond to you the way that you expect or would want them to. You will also definitely meet people who are very hard to predict, and some would even be rude to you. You should be flexible enough to handle all these types of people. This may be hard for beginners, but if you practice enough, then you will soon be able to handle any kind of conversation and people. Talking to people is an art. There is no rule as to how you should respond or react, and there is also no rule as to what you should tell the other person. You are always free to express yourself. Unfortunately, many people are not good at expressing themselves. You should be flexible enough to deal with such kind of people. You may have to be more patient and make some adjustments just to talk with them effectively. Sometimes the art of talking is like a dance where you also need to make some adjustments in order to move harmoniously with another. There is strict rule that will work for all occasions. This is why you need to find your own voice and set your rhythm.

Be respectful

Be respectful at all times. No matter what happens, never allow your temper or emotion to control the conversation. You should always stay calm and relaxed. A good characteristic of any effective communicator is the respect with which he carries himself. By being respectful, the other person will also feel that he should respect you. Now, it is easy to show respect if you are talking to someone who is very kind and nice. But, what if you find yourself dealing with a difficult person, or a person who only wants to get into a debate with you? In such instances, you may find your temper and patience being put the test. During such time, you should remain respectful. Never succumb to anger. As the saying goes, "Always be a gentleman. Not because the other person is a gentleman, but because you are."

Respect is very important to any relationship, even in a conversation of any kind. No matter how the other person treats you, be sure to treat him kindly. Sometimes it is by respecting other people that they will learn how to respect you. Respect can earn respect.

Have an open mind

It is important for you to keep an open mind when you engage in a conversation. When you converse with a person, you may encounter strange and even contradicting ideas. You get to brainstorm ideas with each other. If you do not have an open mind, then some of the ideas may seem very wrong and revolting. But, if you keep an open mind, then you can have a healthy conversation with anyone. Take note that you do not need to convince the other person to adapt your way of thinking. In the same way, you are not expected to agree with everything that the other person is saying. You are always free to disagree. Just remember to express your disagreement politely and respectfully. You need to understand that you disagree with a certain view or opinion but not necessarily with the person. Hence, you can always have respect for a person despite his contradicting and even erroneous views.

Good communicators know that a person is not always what he says when he talks. In fact, many people are not good at expressing themselves. Therefore, it is very important for you to keep an open mind at all times. By having an open mind, you will also be more open to new and interesting ideas. People also like talking to someone who has an open mind. They want to open up to people whom they know will not judge them no matter what they say. This is another important lesson to remember: Having an open mind means not judging a person no matter what he tells you. Instead, what you should do is to try to understand more the other person. You are not there to judge, but to listen. If you cannot listen and sympathize with another, then perhaps it would be better if you do not engage in a conversation. Again, effective communication is not just about you. It is two-way process. Just as there is a time for you to talk, there is also a time for you to listen.

Have a sense of humor

Learn to laugh — laugh even at yourself and your mistakes. If you notice expert communicators, they usually add some humor to their talks. A humor can release some tension and make people feel more comfortable. Therefore, it is a good practice to use some humor from time to time. However, just be sure to use a humor whenever it is proper. Using humor can make a serious conversation to seem lighter. However, keep in mind that there are also times when the setting is completely serious without any place to drop some humor. Make sure to observe proper timing; otherwise, a humor might be taken out of context and be received as an insult.

Adding some humor is not always an easy thing to do. There is also no assurance that the other person will like it. Hence, if you notice that the person whom you are talking to is trying his best to humor you, show your appreciation for his efforts. Of course, you should also do the same favor and try to use a little humor in your conversation. Also, engaging in a very serious conversation for hours can be very boring and can even make you feel exhausted easily. A good humor, especially when followed by a good laugh, can make you feel less stressed and more comfortable. Therefore, whenever possible, try to use some humor in your conversations.

Learn to use pauses

A pause can be a powerful tool in effective communication. A pause can draw more attention, arouse interest, or it can also give emphasis to something. One of the effective communicators who used a pause properly was Adolf Hitler. Hitler used to pause for few seconds before starting his speech. A pause draws attention, and you will be sure that you have all the attention and focus of the audience the moment you start talking. A pause can also be used to build up the suspense and make the conversation more interesting.

You should remember to use pauses wisely and sparingly. Using too many pauses may not be a good idea; therefore, only use it when you have a clear purpose for doing so. If it does not serve a good purpose, then do not apply it.

Focus on the relationship

You need to realize that talking to people is about building a good relationship. It means so much more than just getting a message across or listening to what the other person has to say. Focus on relationship-building. The more that you are able to build a good relationship, the better the conversation will be.

A common mistake is focusing more on the gain that you expect to get from the conversation. This is true, especially when you attend business meetings. Of course, you will not sacrifice the interest of your business. But, you also need to be cautious of projecting an image of being too greedy. People will find it hard to trust you if they notice that you only care about your own interest.

An effective way to build a good relationship is to focus on the interest of the other person. If you talk about something that the other person is interested in, then you will definitely capture his interest, and he will most likely enjoy talking with you. It is not a surprise that business meetings usually end up with talks about golf, cars, and others. When this happens, friendship starts to develop, and a more meaningful relationship takes shape. Also, when you do this, people will usually appreciate it and tend to be more open and friendly.

Continuous practice

Truly learning effective communication takes more than just reading books and theories about it. In order to become an effective communicator, you need to take positive actions and engage in continuous practice. As already stated, you should apply the techniques of effective communication even in your day-to-day conversations. Remember that every conversation you have is another opportunity to apply and improve your communication skills. After some time, all the techniques and habits of effective communication will be a part of who you are as a person. By then, you will realize that communicating effectively is not a difficult task. By improving your character, you also improve your level of communication. In a way, it can be said that learning how to communicate effectively is about learning to become a better person. This is one of the reasons why learning to become a better and effective communicator is highly beneficial. It also improves you as a person. Not to mention, those who can communicate effectively are usually those who get rewarded since they are the ones who excel at what they do.

You cannot just turn into an expert communicator overnight. Even if you read all the books about talking to people, you still need to spend time and efforts to actually learn the techniques. Of course, the only way to learn them is by active and continuous application.

For starters, it is advised that you focus on learning the techniques one at a time. Hence, you might want to focus on active listening before moving on to other techniques and tips. As you improve and get used to the process of effective communication, you can then apply two or more techniques at the same time. Of course, once you get good at this, you should soon be able to use all the techniques at once and handle any kind of conversation effectively and confidently. Speaking about confidence, it is also an important ingredient of effective communication. The more that you practice, the more confident you will be. Unfortunately, many people who try to learn how to talk effectively do not practice enough. Keep this in mind: Actual practice is very important. You need to try to apply the techniques regularly. Also, do not just wait for people to come and talk to you. You should take the initiative and be more social and talk to people. For purpose of practicing the techniques, it is strongly suggested that you make sure to talk to at least one person everyday and be sure to apply the techniques in this book. Do not be discouraged if you are not able to execute them properly. Practice makes perfect, so spend more time practicing the teachings in this book. Soon, you will get used to it and these techniques will be second nature to you that you would not even have to think about them. Instead, they will be a habit that becomes a natural part of who you are. If you watch the videos of expert communicators, you will notice that they are always very relaxed. This is because they do not even think about the techniques. This is because once you reach that level, these techniques are no longer considered techniques but are already a part of who you are as a person. Again, it bears stressing that learning to talk effectively can be a life-changing journey that is full of positive changes.

Conclusion

Thanks for making it through to the end of this book. I hope it was informative and able to provide you with all of the tools you need to achieve your goals whatever they may be.

The next step is to apply everything that you have learned. Learning to talk to people effectively requires continuous practice. It is worth remembering that talking to people is something that is innate in human beings. Hence, do not see the techniques in this book as something difficult to do. Take note that you already have all these skills; you simply have to develop them. If you are just starting out, you may expect to have some difficulty in applying the techniques and tips in this book. This is normal, so do not be discouraged. Just persist in your practice, and you will soon notice some improvements. Learning to communicate more effectively is just like learning any other new skill. Even if you have all the instructions that you may need, it will still take and practice before you can completely learn how to use the techniques properly.

As you may have already noticed by now, there is really no secret to effective communication. It is only about being and acting more human and knowing that you are connecting with another human being. It is by realizing this truth that makes the activity of talking meaningful and valuable. When you talk, you open yourself up to people. Depending on the quality of the words that you say, you either send positive or negative energy out into the world. In the same manner, when you are the receiver and listens to another, you receive whatever the other person is opening up to you. The process of communication is a beautiful exchange that takes place between two or more human beings.

It is worth noting that you should not limit yourself to the techniques in this book, as well as other books on the same subject. Talking effectively to people is an art; therefore, do not let any teaching to put limitation as to how talking should be. Feel free to modify the techniques and even come up with your own set of techniques. Since talking can be considered an art, use it in a way that you express yourself more beautifully and effectively.

As you learn and apply the techniques of effective communication, you will notice some positive changes in your life. Most likely, you will notice how people respond more favorably when you talk to them effectively. You may even make new friends and show excellence in what you do. More importantly, learning how to talk effectively will make you more human and make you conscious of the beauty that comes with connecting to another human being. Unfortunately, since people talk and talk every day, many tend to take things for granted that they fail to see how wonderful it is to connect and talk with another human being. Learning to talk effectively to people will remind you of what truly matters and make you a better human being.

There is joy in being able to talk effectively to people. Indeed, this is a "skill" that is worth learning. By now, you should already have a good foundation and understanding of how to talk to people effectively. Feel free to review the techniques and even come up with your own. More importantly, be sure to apply your knowledge. Effective communication requires continuous practice. Stop being shy or worrying; it is time for you to enjoy connecting with another soul: Talk and connect with another human being.

www.ingramcontent.com/pod-product-compliance
Lightning Source LLC
Chambersburg PA
CBHW060942130726
48001CB00003B/1016